Swift, Simple, Sweet.

W. J. Scott

Cover design and good photography
Andrew Scott

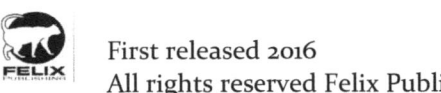

First released 2016
All rights reserved Felix Publishing

Felix Publishing 2016
www.felixpublishing.com.au
email: wjscott@felixpublishing.com
Print copies available from publisher.

Swift, Simple, Sweet.......
2016 digital book release
ISBN: 978-0-9945755-3-1

Author: W.J. Scott
Cover and some photography Andrew Scott

Other books by W. J. Scott in this series:
Make Life Simpler

The Perfect Assignment
ISBN: 978-0-9945755-0-0

Debt Free, The Morals of Money Management
ISBN: 978-0-9945755-2-4

Libre de Deuda, de la moral de la administración del dinero
ISBN: 978-0-9945755-1-7

Registration:
Thorpe-Bowker +61 3 8517 8342
email: bowkerlink@thorpe.com.au
No part of this publication may be reproduced, stored in a retrieval system, or transmitted in any form or by any means, electronic, mechanical, photocopying, recording or otherwise, without the prior written permission of the publisher.

 © All rights reserved Felix Publishing

INTRODUCTION

WARNING

I am not a trained cook or chef. I have however been cooking with various levels of success for over 45 years. I did get lots of guidance from the ladies in the CWA when I lived in the country. So far nobody has died from eating my food, and some even like it. All my recipes are the lowest fat, salt and sugar variations. If you want more add more. I rarely add salt to cooking; it is added at the table if others want it.

All instructions will be the quickest way to get good results, standard cook books will choose the way to get perhaps perfect results that may or may not happen, but will involve more mixing bowls, more time and usually more expensive ingredients.

CONTENTS

Scones (biscuits) 5
Damper 8
Cakes 9
Fruitcake 12
Fast icings 14
Muffins 15
Biscuits (cookies) 18
Gingerbread Men and Ladies 20
Desserts 23
Chocolate Ripple Ice Cream Log 27
Smoothies 33
Quick Chocolate Toppings 35
Quiche 36
Magic Mince 38
Meat 42
Stir Fry 48
Pasta 49
Vegetables 54
Salads 56
Bring a Plate Sweet 59
Bring a Plate Savoury 63
Breakfast 69
Cooking for Food Intolerances 78
Converting Recipes to Low Fat / Low Sat 81
Faster Still 83
Getting Children to Eat without Tears, Yours or Theirs 85
Your Own Recipes 91

SCONES

Basic scones (American biscuits) are all variations of flour, butter and milk in roughly the following proportions:

2 cups of self-raising flour
¾ cup milk (or other liquid)
60 grams butter

You will note that the total liquid, including the butter, gets to 1 cup and dry ingredients 2 cups. When adding your personal touches keep roughly to this. Powdered milk or a substitute is just fine.

All recipes will tell you to rub the butter through with your fingertips into the flour and then gently fold in the milk until you get a soft dough. All recipes but this one. Let's speed things up.

Melt the butter/ margarine/ substitute in the microwave for 10 seconds.

Now before you do anything else set the oven to 220°C, down a bit for fan forced electric.

Put the flour in a mixing bowl, pour in the slightly cooled butter, and give it a quick stir with a spoon until it looks like crumbs now pour in most, not all of the milk. Stir until a dough forms, add more milk if needed for a soft but not sloppy dough.

Throw lots of flour on a board; knead into shape for about 10 seconds. Use only finger tips or it will be too heavy (cricket balls).

Squish to about 2 cm high now cut out the scones and place touching each other on a greased oven tray. Brush the tops with milk, and a sprinkle of sugar if wished or beaten egg.

Pop it into the oven until risen and light brown on top. The ones in the photo are a little well done, but that is life! They tasted good with butter and jam, or jam and cream.

This should take about 10-15 minutes depending on your oven.

This whole procedure took 20 minutes of your life that you will not get back.

I hope you doubled the mixture so you have lots of 6 packs in sandwich bags in the freezer for when you only want to boil the jug and nuke the just fresh hot scones for 20 seconds in the microwave.

Remember presentation! Classy china works well as shown. A dab of flour on your nose is good too. Put the tea in a pot, if you must use a tea bag pull it out before serving or make sure there are no strings hanging out of the pot.

Variations:

Sultanas, a generous handful before adding milk

Dates, chop well, a generous handful before adding milk

Pumpkin, cook 1 cup pumpkin and mash it in some of the cooking water, when cooled a little melt the butter in the pumpkin, then cool some more before adding a lightly whisked egg, then add the flour.

Add milk only if there was not enough pumpkin water. This is a softer dough.

My favourite, add ½ cup grated cheese, 1 tablespoon finely chopped capsicum (bell pepper), ½ finely chopped small onion, tablespoon of mixed herbs, tablespoon of corn, 1 tablespoon peas, you may need extra milk.

Damper

Replace butter with 2 tablespoons oil, replace milk with water and add some salt. Put the whole blob, after kneading, on a greased tray and score the surface with a knife into wedges keeping the height to about 5 cm. Brush top with oil, water or milk. Good when camping as a bread replacement, works well with soup and lots of butter.

To warm up those you have frozen, slightly dampen paper towel wrap the scones 2-6 at a time and spread them round the edge of a round side plate and give them 20-30 seconds on medium to high. Do not use fancy plates in the microwave!

CAKES

Most standard cakes are a variation of this. The same mass of butter and sugar and twice the amount of flour with eggs and milk. There are also basic sponge recipes and fruitcake, boiled or cooked forever. As you, like me, probably do not want to spend your life just in the kitchen, one basic fast recipe with variations will do and look up any specific recipe if you feel the need.

125g butter/ margarine/ substitute
125g sugar/ white/raw/caster/fake stuff as if!
250g self-raising flour
2 eggs
½ cup milk

Note butter + sugar = flour   eggs = milk volume

Grandma's way with a wooden spoon beat the butter and sugar together until creamy, 10-15 minutes add the eggs and a splash of vanilla and beat well stir in milk mix and add the flour gradually to avoid lumps.........well done if you do.

How about melt butter in microwave~20 seconds pour it over sugar stir in with mixer, add everything except flour, and beat it.

Add flour on low until no lumps. Pour into greased cake tin or patty pans with cake papers, or muffin or cupcake trays.

Cook in a pre-heated, moderate oven until light brown and springs back when gently pressed in the middle. Cool on a rack totally before icing.

If the top is dodgy, up end the cake and ice the top!

Variations:

Chocolate, add a couple of tablespoons of good cocoa powder, not drink mix, and a splash more liquid to make up for the extra dry ingredients.

Sultana, put a handful of sultanas into the flour flick them around so they coat thoroughly or they will sink to the bottom.

Strawberry, pink colour and a few drops of flavouring.

Marble cake, this looks impressive divide the mix in 3, tint one pink with flavouring, leave one as vanilla, and stir the cocoa into the third.
Now put tablespoons of each in random patterns over the bottom of the cake tin then repeat until all is used up. Use a knife or skewer to do a swirly pattern through the batter, not too much or the colours will not stay separate.

Layer cakes, pour the batter into 2 or three cake tins the same size to cook and put fresh whipped cream or icing or filling between layers. Then ice the top.

Vanilla cake in 2 layers with the bottom layer spread with a berry jam then whipped cream, the top layer then has a doily laid on top and icing sugar sprinkled over. The doily is carefully removed (this is best done lightly and with a paper doily as it is stiffer) and the pattern in icing sugar looks really impressive.

Alternatively there are some very good packet mixes available, you cook and decorate, job done. Supermarkets also sell sponges ready to decorate if you are in a real hurry and do not want the smell of cooking cakes in the house.

Fruitcake for the culinarily lazy, or for those who have a life.

Fruitcake, fast and furious, almost anything can be substituted.

Muffin or patty cake size are ideal as they cook quickest and are ideal to freeze for small households, also there is no messy crumbling when you hack into the big cake to get your extra slices. Mini muffin size is perfect for diet conscious or children, satisfying and tasty treat without interfering with the next meal.

1kg home brand mixed fruit (or any combination of dried fruit you like)
600ml carton of chocolate milk (use real or fake milk of any sort, and 2-3 tablespoons of topping of choice)
2 cups self-raising flour (or whatever substitute you use)
1-3 tablespoons of spices of choice, I use ginger, nutmeg and cinnamon, or leave it out entirely

In a big bowl throw in dried fruit, break it up a little so it is not in one chunk, pour over carton of milk. Put it in the fridge overnight, enough work for one day!

Next day throw in flour and spices stir with a spoon until all is wet, maybe 20 seconds.

Preheat oven to 160°C

Spray muffin pans or large cake tins, drop in the mix and cook until light brown and a skewer comes out clean, 12-15 mins for muffin size, just over an hour for big cake.

Make a cup of tea to enjoy with the cake, you deserve it after all that work.

Fast Icings

Fondant icings are available ready to roll out and trim. There are also tubs of icing ready to spread or pipe or both.

Royal icing with pure icing sugar and egg white takes forever but looks and tastes really good. If you have neither time nor inclination use the fondant.

Glazed icing. A cup of icing sugar mix and a teaspoon of water or juice, mix firmly add extra liquid drop by drop you do not want it runny it will never set. As soon as it is spreadable stop. Add a few drops of colour if wanted *before* the liquid. Spread it over the cake with a knife.

Chocolate icing use glazed with a little cocoa powder, or if you are really lazy Nutella is fine.

Fluffy butter frosting is my favourite, add a teaspoon of butter or substitute to every cup of icing sugar mix a drop of vanilla belt the living daylights out of it and then as little milk as you can flick it around and you have a lovely soft icing for decorating. This is easily coloured and can be used as filling as well as icing.

MUFFINS

Guess what! There is a one size fits all recipe for this.

Muffins are more fun to make because you just need a fork and a spoon to mix. Too much mixing makes them very rubbery.

These muffins are much healthier than cakes but taste just as good.

1/3 cup oil   not olive it has too strong a flavour.
1/3 cup sugar
1 cup of milk
2 cups self-raising flour
2 eggs

Set the oven to moderately hot about 190 degrees C give or take, depending on whether it is fan forced, gas or electric etc.

Flick through the oil, milk, eggs and sugar until all evenly coloured. Stir through the flour until just mixed and all the flour is wet.

Grease muffin pans, mini muffins are great for a snack, patty pan size are good for morning tea, and Texas muffins are a main meal!

Spoon the mixture into muffin pans having mixture just under ¾ full. Cook until light brown and bounce back when pressed in the centre.

Pictured: blueberry muffins and raspberry chocolate chip mini muffins

Variations:

Chocolate chips, add a hand full or more in with flour.

Fruit, mix dried fruit in with flour before adding.

Orange and poppy seed, finely grated rind of orange, lemon or lime and about ¼ cup poppy seeds.

Cherry, coconut and chocolate chip. Very impressive, glace cherries, ½ cup coconut and chocolate chips.

Banana, mash it and add a little more flour.

Grated cheese and chives, leave out the sugar.

Cheese, herbs and capsicum very yummy no sugar.

With the additions of moist ingredients add a little more flour, if there are a lot of dry ingredients add a little more milk, have fun designing your own.

They freeze very well. They take 5 minutes to thaw on a plate on the bench.

BISCUITS

If you are American these are cookies.

Like cakes there is a basic recipe that you can vary to your heart's delight.

It is basically the cake recipe without the second egg and milk, how hard is that?

125g butter/ margarine/substitute
125g sugar/ white/ caster/ raw/dare I say substitute?
250g self-raising flour
1 egg

Grandma's way cream butter and sugar...................as if you will!

Melt butter in microwave or on the bench in Australian summer, add sugar, mix add vanilla, and egg beat it lightly, then stir in flour.

Roll teaspoons of dough and drop onto a greased oven tray, squish top a little with a fork, or not.

Leave room for lots of spreading.

Cook in a moderate oven until brown.
Cool on a rack and store in an airtight container.

Obviously you will make at least a double batch to freeze for later.

Variations:

Jam drops use a round handled wooden spoon or similar to push little dents into the centre of the biscuit dough on the baking tray, put little blobs of jam inside the hollow. Bake as usual. If you overfill the jam it spreads everywhere and looks awful.

Coconut is mixed in dough first or roll dough ball in coconut before baking, lightly squish with fork.

Chocolate chip throw in lots of chocolate chips in with the flour.

Dried fruit chopped finely or whole sultanas are nice.

Chocolate, use a tablespoon or two of cocoa powder in with the flour.

Chocolate coated: melt 200g dark cooking chocolate, all broken into little pieces (30 seconds in the microwave, note it will keep its shape so stir to check), or put in a heatproof bowl over a pot of boiling water, now do not let the steam get in the chocolate or it will be ruined (hey you might do it the slow way, I am just giving choices,) stir in 1 tablespoon cooking oil (not olive oil the flavour is too strong). Now dip the cooked, cooled biscuits in or spread it over with a knife.

Use your imagination.

To use a biscuit forcer to squirt out lovely shaped biscuits add 1 tablespoon of milk to the recipe to make it the right consistency, keep to plain or chocolate using cocoa powder for that.

To cut out biscuits add a little more flour to make a firmer mixture, ginger and spices always smell and taste good, use raw sugar with ginger or golden syrup. Use more spice than you think you need or they will be very bland.

Gingerbread Men and Ladies

125g butter
½ cup raw sugar
1 egg a big one
½ cup golden syrup
1 heaped tablespoon ginger
1 teaspoon nutmeg
1 teaspoon cinnamon
1 teaspoon bicarbonate of soda
2 ½ cups plain flour

Melt butter in microwave, stir in sugar, golden syrup then beat through the egg.
Stir in the flour, spices and bicarb together into the wet ingredients. Knead for a few seconds until pliable and even.

Wrap in cling wrap and put into the fridge for 30 minutes while you have a cup of tea and put your feet up. Miss this step and the biscuits will not hold together well.

Roll out dough and cut with cutters. Put onto a greased oven tray. It takes about 10 minutes to cook on 180°C. It also takes about 10 minutes to cut the biscuits out for a full large tray.

Let them cool on a rack. When very cold ice with icing sugar and a few drops of water, lollies (candy), jelly snakes cut up, and toothpicks dipped in food colour to draw.

Get the whole family involved. They take 25 minutes plus 30 mins in the fridge plus icing time but you get about 36-48 if you make them using small to medium sized cutters. That is an awful lot of morning teas.

DESSERTS

Cheat's Christmas pudding:

Buy a supermarket dark fruit cake. Dispose of the wrapping in the outside bin. Cut the cake into large cubes, enough for everyone to have one.

If you indulge - splash a little rum, sherry, or grog of your choice (not for the young ones) on the cubes before heating in the microwave for a few seconds.

Serve with hot or cold custard poured over, bought or homemade, a little squirt of cream on top and a cherry and you have a very fancy dessert.

Remember presentation and confidence.

2 minute custard:

600ml boiling water in a microwave jug let it cool for as long as it takes to assemble the other ingredients.
4-6 heaped tablespoons of powdered milk
2 tablespoons custard powder
2 tablespoons of cold water
2 tablespoons of sugar

Using a balloon whisk, whisk the powdered milk, sugar and hot water together. In a cup stir custard powder and cold water until it is runny not stiff.

Pour into jug and whisk. The whisk gets rid of lumps, use a spoon if you never get lumps.

Microwave for 30 seconds. Whisk, if thick all over bring it out ready to serve, if not give it another 30 seconds, repeat up to 4 times.

Serve hot or cold with sliced bananas, with jelly (jello), cake and fruit for a trifle, pour it over any other dessert or serve it plain with a little cinnamon or nutmeg on top. For Christmas puddings or entertaining put it into a fancy jug and let guests serve themselves.

Ginger nut biscuit (photo), microwaved and pushed into tartlet baking tray, before and after filling. Before whipped cream if desired.

Caramel tarts (about 5 minutes plus chill time)
1 packet of ginger nut biscuits (cheaper brands have less fat and sugar and work best).
1 tin caramel,
Whipped cream
Mini tart tray / patty cake tray with a rounded base

Microwave 4-6 biscuits at a time for 20 seconds, working quickly whilst they are hot and soft squish them gently into the tray. Continue until all of the biscuits are in the tray. Open the tin and put a heaped teaspoon of caramel in each tart, smooth it with the back of a spoon. Pop it into the fridge for at least 30 minutes. Serve on a pretty plate with a dollop of whipped cream if wanted. Trust me these disappear in minutes.

Variations:

Use lemon butter, or **chocolate filling**, or **Nutella**, or **pureed fruit** that is thickened, let your imagination run wild.

Plain coconut or butternut style biscuits also work well if you do not like ginger or want a change. The children can definitely make these if you do the microwaving. These tarts are also very, very popular for bring a plate. Whenever I serve these I am asked for the recipe. You can honestly say these are just something I whipped up this afternoon when I heard you were coming over.

CHOCOLATE RIPPLE ICE CREAM LOG

Chocolate Ripple Ice cream Log 5 minutes preparation

2 litres vanilla ice cream
1 packet plain chocolate flavoured biscuits, not chocolate coated.
Loaf tin or similar

Line the loaf tin with cling wrap or foil leaving it hanging over the sides so you can lift out the dessert.

Spoon out some ice cream and spread a layer about 2cm deep in the tin. Open the packet of biscuits. Now using the ice cream as spread, thickly spread the first biscuit on both sides and stand it up at one end of the tin in the ice cream layer.

Next spread one side of the next biscuit and press it against the first and into the ice cream, keep going in this manner until you are almost at the end of the tin. Now spread ice cream over both ends and over the top and sides to totally enclose the tube of ice cream coated biscuits.

Bring the cling wrap over the top and gently smooth it into a swiss roll shape. Put the tin in the freezer for at least an hour.

When ready to serve, lift it out of the tin and place it on a glass or fancy long serving dish. Do diagonal cuts and serve in slices so everyone gets the soft cake (yes it looks and tastes like cake) stripes in the ice cream. Pretty up the plate if you wish with mint leaves, whipped cream or strawberries thinly sliced to the hull and fanned out. Very pretty. Or if you have teenagers they will just wolf down the lot without the decoration.

Banana Split

Ice cream, 2 scoops per person
1 small or ½ large banana per person
Syrup
Nuts/sprinkles
Ice cream wafers
Pretty dessert bowls here. Cut the bananas lengthwise, put on 2 scoops of ice cream, pour over syrup of choice or melted chocolate topping from earlier in this book, sprinkle crushed nuts or sprinkles. Diagonally cut the ice cream wafers and poke the two halves in elegantly serve immediately. Diet version is smaller prettier glass bowls preferably with stem, ½ banana, 1 scoop of low fat ice cream, 1 passionfruit or fanned strawberry over the top and leave off the wafer. Calories and kilojoules cut to a third of the other version.

Fresh fruit

A wedge of pineapple cut lengthwise then with vertical cuts to skin, and a long cut from tip to tip against the skin the little wedges can be picked up with toothpicks at a party or fork or fingers at home.

Mangoes cut the cheeks off touching the stone, then score with parallel cuts from end to end and across. About 3 cuts in each direction giving squares. Then fold the fruit backwards and the cubes stand proud easy to eat without a mess.

Oranges are easy to eat if they are cut into wedges, about 8 per orange.

Bananas just cut off the stem and they are easy to peel as soon as someone is hungry.

Grapes, little bunches of 6-8 grapes work best.

Apples, adults can just eat them unless it is a fruit salad platter in which case, cut them into 8 wedges and remove the core. If preparing beforehand wipe over with orange juice so they do not turn brown.

SMOOTHIES

Wonderful in hot weather when you do not feel like eating. I use 385ml glasses they are much bigger than the standard 250ml cup or glass. Adjust accordingly.

When you have fruit in season in abundance, freeze it for later use. Bananas, throw in freezer with skin on, as is. Mangoes chop and add 1/3 water before blending then pour into ice cube trays. Oranges, lemons peel, chop blend with 1/3 water, strawberries and other berries chop and blend with 1/3 water. Freeze in ice cube trays, next day when set put in labelled freezer bags or plastic containers.

Mango
½ glass (200ml) milk
Half chopped mango
Blend with 2 ice cubes.

Banana
½ glass milk
1 medium banana
Blend with 2 ice cubes

Mango and banana
200ml milk
½ banana
1/4 mango
Blend with 2 ice cubes.

See the pattern here - pick any soft fruit.

If using the previously frozen pureed fruit - 3 mango cubes with ½ banana 200ml milk this makes it extra fluffy and it is extra refreshing.

Thick shake texture.

You can use a tablespoon of yoghurt with any of the milk based smoothies.

You can also make the smoothies without milk, the South Americans call this jugo and it tastes lovely. The lemon version is often served at meals.

1 chopped orange
1 slice of pineapple
3 ice cubes
100ml of water to blend

Again any soft fruit that takes your fancy go for it. The ice cubes or frozen puree cubes make it very fluffy.

QUICK CHOCOLATE TOPPINGS

100grams dark cooking chocolate
1 tablespoon of oil

Break the chocolate into squares and
1. put it into a double boiler and keep it away from steam to melt (you could do that, it is recommended)
or 2. Put in small microwaveable jug and melt for 20-30 seconds.

Stir in the oil until smooth, about 10 seconds.

This is the hard crackly chocolate on a chocolate coated ice cream from the cinemas, and the expensive individually wrapped ones in various shapes. Pour it straight over ice cream in a bowl or cone, sprinkle on nuts or hundreds and thousands if you wish.

For a thick ganache on top of a cake use 2 tablespoons of cream instead of the oil.

QUICHE

You can make quiche by making pastry from scratch, blind baking the case then carefully layering all the filling and then baking in the oven until set. Apart from using every bowl in the kitchen and taking half a day it will be high fat and less healthy. You could also make a quiche by bunging everything in the one bowl stirring it around, then pouring into dish to cook. For the first you need to look to those glossy books written by chefs, and really love cooking, for the latter read on. Fast, fabulous and healthy!

Get a big mixing bowl, a large spoon and we are ready. Turn oven to moderate, about 175°C

¾ cup plain flour
2 tablespoons of butter or margarine melted or cooking oil
2 tablespoons of oat bran
½ cup processed bran (All bran or better still the no name equivalent with less salt and additives)
4 large eggs
2 cups of milk (powdered skim milk double strength makes it extra creamy, lower fat)
Small tin tuna in spring water drained or hand full of chopped bacon or cold chicken chopped, or any leftover meat, or none.
2 cups of chopped left over vegetables, and or frozen vegetables, or just asparagus and onion, or just tomatoes and onion, or whatever you feel like.

½ cup grated cheese low fat by choice.

How to:
Put flour and oil/ butter in the bowl stir around until all crumbly looking, throw in the bran.
Mix the milk and eggs before pouring in, ideal, or not and give them a flick around when they get into the bowl without stirring the flour, that is a bit harder.
Now throw everything else in on top. Stir with the big spoon until mixed through.

Grease a quiche dish, or ramekins if you live alone, or want individual quiches, or spray oil into small muffin trays if you want them as party food (not mini, not Texas size) pour mix in to half way up the sides.

Pop into oven until they are set and lightly browned. Time depends upon the size, 10-15 minutes for tiny, 20-30 for individual and 35-45 for large.

Common sense says you do a double batch to fill the freezer and save on power. There will be lots of days when you are busy, sick, sick of cooking, or have unexpected guests when having a meal ready in the freezer that is healthy and tastes great. It beats a horrible greasy take away and saves the credit card from meltdown.

Serve with a side salad and dinner is ready.

MAGIC MINCE

Meatloaf:

500g low fat beef mince
1 large onion finely chopped
1 tablespoon mixed herbs
1 large or 2 small carrots grated
Grated zucchini (courgettes)
Finely chopped ½ capsicum (bell pepper)
1 egg
1 cup bread crumbs /or oats or /2 weetbix crumbled

Scrub your hands more thoroughly than usual, throw all ingredients in a mixing bowl and squish together with your hands, or get the children to do it. Throw the blob in a loaf pan and cook in a moderate oven, 175-185°C until brown on the top and cooked through. Serve hot with steamed vegetables or salad. Also good cold.

Variations:

Swap beef for lamb with mint, or chicken.

Vegetarian mince, if using dried soy mince or similar add a little oil and a dessertspoon of vegemite. If using tinned varieties just do a direct substitute.

Throw in all your leftover cooked vegetables, either chopped up or mashed if you are hiding them from the children.

Add chopped tomatoes and basil, oregano and a little minced garlic.

Small tin crushed pineapple no sugar, drained, chopped mint leaves, pour reserved juice over the top as a glaze when cooking.

Visitors are coming, use the pineapple above or boil 3 eggs, peel them and lay them on 1/3 mince mixture in the tin, cover carefully with the rest. Do not leave any air gaps.

Meatballs:

Use a variation of the meatloaf mixture roll into little balls, the size of walnuts for on pasta or egg size for rissoles. Dry fry or use spray oil in a pan.

For minimum effort just use the mince and a few herbs rolled into balls. Add the grated carrot and onion and others for flavour, the bread crumbs are to hold it together with the egg. These are left out for gluten or egg allergies.

Spaghetti Bolognese sauce:

500g beef mince
2 onions finely chopped
1 teaspoon minced garlic
1 good beef cube or 2 cheap ones
1 teaspoon basil dried or 3 teaspoons fresh
1 teaspoon oregano dried or 3 teaspoons fresh
700ml bottle of tomato passata (tomato puree)

Brown the mince and onion, throw everything else in and simmer until cooked through, about 5 minutes. Pour over pasta of choice, or use as the beef layer in lasagna. Mince can be used when thickened in pies or in jaffles or spiced up for tacos. When you make this, divide the mix for multiple uses. Use some - freeze some.

Koi Sim:

Get a big boiler/ pot with 1 tablespoon oil ready and add the ingredients in order as you chop them. Put rice on to cook here too. Expect 15 minutes cooking time total.

500g mince, brown with
2 finely chopped onions
Then add 2 grated carrots
1 grated apple
Packet chicken noodle soup with 2 cups water
1 beef cube
1 tablespoon curry powder

1 tablespoon mustard powder
2 tablespoons soy sauce
Finely shredded ¼ cabbage

Simmer about 5 minutes until cabbage is soft. Serve with steamed rice. Even my Chinese neighbours love this.

MEAT

Grills: 12 minutes from hot griller to table!

Steak, use a good cut for grilling or it will be tough.
Steak, size of a pack of cards per adult (half for child, twice for fast growing teens).

1 tomato per person
Oven chips if wanted
Lettuce cucumber etc. for side salad
Bread stick or garlic bread if wanted

Set the grill fairly high, brown one side to seal the juices in, turn it over and finish the other side. Rare is while it still bleeds when poked with tongs and is soft. Well done is very dark not black and does not dent when poked with tongs and no liquid oozes out. Probably best to aim for somewhere in between. It should take about 10 minutes. That is ample time for tastefully arranging salad on the plates ready for the meat. Crusty bread or garlic bread are nice on the side.

If you slice a tomato in half and sprinkle mixed herbs and grated cheese on top this is lovely with the grill and cooks in slightly less time so you prepare it after throwing the meat on the grill.

You can cheat chips to go with it as well, get frozen oven fry chips and throw them on the grill with the meat and turn at the same time.

The recommended serve of red meat is the size of the palm of your hand and 1 cm thick or the size of a pack of cards. Larger than this is not recommended for your health's sake. If you feel the need for larger serves have chicken or fish where the recommended serve is twice that size for an adult.

12 minutes from having the ingredients on the bench to a healthy nice looking and substantial meal. Serve with a banana split to add extra fruit and calcium.

Variations:

Chops, lamb loin or shoulder for a larger size, not neck they are for stewing.

Chicken breast, legs or thighs a squeeze of lemon and pepper is nice whilst grilling

Fish fillet, again lemon is nice, serve lemon wedges on the side

Rissoles are lower fat when grilled

Sausages

Fish fingers

Fish cakes, pre made (homemade are best dry fried)

ROASTS

Lamb roast in frying pan still cooking (pictured)

Sunday roast

Lamb

Lamb roast, leg, or half leg, shoulder
Potatoes
Sweet potatoes (yams)
Pumpkin
Carrots
Peas / beans / broccoli / snow peas / Brussel sprouts
Gravy mix or plain flour and salt.

Set oven for 180°C or my preferred electric frying pan on medium. Spray the baking dish or frying pan with oil, lower in roast, and seal (brown) on one side then roll over and seal the other side. Allow cooking time of about an hour per 1kg weight of the meat. Now sit down and read the Sunday paper, every 20 minutes roll the roast.

Peel the vegetables, cut into cubes about 4cm side. Carrots can be cut into sticks and boiled with the green veg if preferred. Throw the vegetables into the frying pan 45 minutes before roast is cooked. Spray with oil, and turn about every 10-15 minutes. Check if they are tender with a fork. They should be nicely browned. The photo is about 15 minutes before the roast is ready.

15 minutes before the roast is cooked put carrot sticks and green vegetables in to boil. Watch that they do not overcook. Bright green is good, khaki or brown is bad.

Put roast on carving tray to rest, remove roast vegetables from pan, leave about 2 tablespoons of oil in the pan, add 2 tablespoons of gravy mix or flour and salt, stir until brown and thick, add about 1 cup of water and bring it to the boil whilst stirring. Season to taste. Or skip this bit and use instant gravy that you make in a cup with boiling water or open a liquid sachet and warm in the microwave.

Special roast:

1 tablespoon of Dijon or similar mustard
1 tablespoon of butter
1 tablespoon of honey
A good handful of fresh rosemary

Break the rosemary into little 2 cm trees and poke into roast all over, save about half of the rosemary leaves, no stalks and mix with the other ingredients. Mix into a paste and smear all over the roast. Now follow all the instructions for the standard roast.

Now carve the roast and serve the vegetables and gravy.

Variations:

Chicken, either whole or pieces

Whole fish

Rolled roast beef

Silverside whole beef roast

Cheats method:

Get an oven bag, insert roast, and sprinkle with appropriate flavour cup of soup (dry). Pierce the oven bag after tying off. Sit on microwave safe plate. Cut cooking time to 8 minutes per kg. Roll over at 3 minute intervals. Watch it! Ovens vary greatly. Peel the vegetables and cut as directed then put in the bag for the last 5 minutes.

For normal roast you can par boil the potatoes, pumpkin and sweet potatoes and just finish the last 10 minutes in the pan.

STIR FRY

Fast fun and healthy, it ticks all the boxes!

Chicken, beef, lamb, pork cut in thin strips or tofu cut in cubes.
Onions cut into wedges
Celery cut into diagonal pieces
Capsicum cut in strips
Snow peas/ beans/ any veg in the fridge
Carrots cut thinly any shape that will cook quickly no chunks
Bok choy, or any Chinese green vegetable or cabbage chopped

Heat 1 tablespoon of oil in the wok or big frying pan. Throw in the meat and onions first, keep stirring so it doesn't burn. Remove from pan and continue with the vegetables, when almost cooked throw everything back in the pan add 1 tablespoon honey, 2 tablespoons soy sauce, sesame seeds, stir for about 1 minute. Serve with 2 minute noodles.

Variations:

Add slivers of ginger, crushed garlic, coriander or whatever is left over. Cold cooked meat can substitute for raw, just leave out step 1.

PASTA

Spaghetti Bolognese

Use sauce from magic mince, and follow pack directions to cook the pasta, serve with grated parmesan cheese. Spirals, bows or whatever shape you like do not just use spaghetti. For children who do not like vegetables or just do not want to eat them, hide lots of grated or finely chopped vegetables in the pasta sauce.

Macaroni Cheese

Cook macaroni as per packet directions.
Cheese sauce
Optional sauté a finely chopped onion in butter or substitute.

Heat 500ml milk or (boil jug and dissolve 6-8 heaped tablespoons skim milk powder in 500ml water)

Mix 2 tablespoons corn flour in 2 tablespoons water to form paste

Stir corn flour into hot milk, add onions if using.
Microwave 1 minute, stir thoroughly or stir in pot on stove top until thickened.

Add 1 cup grated cheese stir through.

Layer macaroni and cheese sauce with sliced tomatoes, top with grated cheese and brown top in oven.

Mornays

Cook the pasta of your choice. Make a standard cheese sauce (in macaroni cheese recipe) with sautéed onion and throw in a small tin of tuna. Serve as is with salad or vegetables or throw the lot in the oven in a casserole dish with grated cheese on top and brown. Nicer this way when you have all the bowls on the table for serve yourself.

Lasagne

Grease a casserole dish, layer uncooked pasta sheets with spaghetti bolognese mince then a layer of cheese sauce, then more pasta, mince, cheese sauce, keep going until you run out of pasta or room in the dish. The top layer is pasta with a little cheese sauce spread over and topped with grated cheese. Cook in moderate oven about half an hour until the pasta is cooked, then turn the oven up to brown the cheese. Best to make two at once if you want one in the freezer as this will disappear very quickly.

High Speed Cannelloni

This is a variation of a dish my son invented for when he was too tired after cooking all day and night for others but was very hungry and needed comfort food. This is ideal for unexpected guests or friends or family drop by and decide to stay for dinner and company. You want time with them not with the stove. Keep a spare bag of the dim sims and grated cheese in the freezer and passata and diced tomatoes in the cupboard. This recipe serves 8-10 adults or 5 very hungry teenagers.

1 packet of home brand dim sims (1.5kg bag has 30 pieces) less than $4
700ml bottle of passata
1 tin diced tomatoes
1 diced onion
2 teaspoons minced garlic (in the bottle)
1 big handful of fresh basil and oregano (or 2 tablespoons of dried)
1 cup of grated cheese

Boil dim sims for about 5 minutes until soft. Sauté onions in 1 teaspoon of butter in the microwave for 30 seconds. Get a very large baking dish that will not look shabby on the table , or a couple of casserole dishes, grease them and neatly lay the dim sims almost touching so they are easy to separate later. Keep to an orderly pattern. Now pour over the passata, garlic, onions, herbs, and chopped tomatoes that you have lightly stirred for a few seconds to mix. Sprinkle the grated cheese on top and put in a moderate oven, about 180°C. Take out a pretty bowl of crisps and drinks to share and join your guests for 25 minutes. Serve with salad and crusty bread.

Pizza with Attitude

Buy a pizza base/ or use scone dough/ or use pita bread or half muffins or bread cut into circles with egg rings or scone cutters. Always use wholemeal if it is available.
Or make it fast base:

2 cups self-raising flour
1 cup Greek yoghurt
Stir together, knead about 20 seconds, divide dough into two. Roll each into a ball, throw to the centre of an oven tray or pizza tray, squish or roll into a circle. Done! It gets cooked in the same time as the topping.

Tomato paste or a bottle of passata (tomato puree with no additives usually near spaghetti sauce bottles)
Minced garlic
Basil
Oregano
Bacon, ham, chicken, meatloaf, mushrooms, sausages (basically whatever is in the fridge chopped up)
Onion, capsicum any and all colours, pineapple, zucchini, and any leftover cooked vegetables from the fridge
Bag grated cheese

Grease oven tray or pizza tray if you have one (serious cooks do, those who love cooking).

Put pizza base or substitute on it, if raw part cook it.
Mix tomato paste, garlic, herbs together and spread generously over base.

Then throw everything else on try to get an even spread of everything, shower cheese over the top. Be generous. Put in the oven about 190° C. When the cheese is melted and browned call the tribe in for dinner. If desired serve with tossed salad and crusty bread.

VEGETABLES

Steamed vegetables are a lovely balance to a very spicy meat dish, or with a very delicately flavoured fish that you do not wish to overpower with spicy vegetables. Clean the vegetables and peel if desired, cut into preferred size and shape then steam until tender not soft. Keep up lots of colour to add interest and balance.

Tomatoes are very nice when split in half and sprinkled with basil, oregano and grated cheese before grilling. This is ideal with grilled meat, less washing up less power, and a good balance of flavours.

Greek style vegetables:

1 large onion cut into wedges
2 medium zucchini cut in thick slices
2 very ripe tomatoes cut in thick wedges
1 clove of garlic crushed, or a teaspoon of minced garlic
Parmesan cheese grated.

Sauté the onion in olive oil then add zucchini to the pan to brown on medium. Add the tomatoes and basil and oregano if wished. Stir around then put the lid on the pan for about 5 minutes until all is tender. Serve with grated parmesan cheese on top, fresh is best but packet works. This is great with a grill and jacket potatoes.

Ratatouille

This is the only vegetable dish that I cook that takes more than 20 minutes in the kitchen but it is well worth it. This is a vegetarian meal in itself. I usually make enough for a couple of meals so the amounts are fairly large.

1 butternut pumpkin or 1 1/2 kg other types cut in 3cm cubes
3 large potatoes peeled and cubed
2 large onions cut in wedges
3 cloves garlic or 3 teaspoons garlic mince
Red and green capsicum cut in thick slices
4 ripe tomatoes cut in chunks
Eggplant (aubergine) cut in 2 cm cubes
3 zucchini (courgettes) sliced thickly
A large handful of fresh basil leaves and oregano torn
Tin chopped tomatoes.

In a moderate oven (electric frying pan is a little faster and less washing up) oil a baking dish, and put pumpkin, eggplant, potato, onion, garlic and capsicum in to roast. Spray oil over the top. After 10 minutes turn the vegetables over. Throw in the herbs 10 minutes later and the rest of the ingredients. Simmer until all of the vegetables are tender. Serve with crusty wholemeal baguettes.

SALADS

Simpler it is the better it tastes.

Tossed salad:

Lettuce, cucumber, English spinach, spring onions, celery, tomatoes.

Break the lettuce into chunks, coarsely cut the other vegetables, and toss together. Add or leave out any of the vegetables. Have salad dressing nearby for anyone who wants to add it to their plate.

Green salad, see above leave out the tomatoes.

Coleslaw:
¼ small cabbage finely shredded
1 large carrot finely grated.

Coleslaw dressing

Toss together and mix until evenly distributed with your own dressing recipe or buy one with your preferred ingredients, don't use too much dressing but do not leave it dry either. You can add finely grated orange zest, shallots, capsicum or whatever you feel like, just try to limit the ingredients as the taste could be overwhelming.

Potato salad:

1 kg boiled potatoes (if big peel them if tiny cook in jackets)
Mayonnaise buy it or make it
Mint leaves

Chop cooked potatoes to preferred size, tear up mint, and toss through mayonnaise. You can add chopped crisp bacon, cut up boiled eggs, peas, again whatever tastes nice to you.

Pasta salad:

Your choice of small pasta cooked, I prefer small shells
Red and green capsicum finely chopped
Mayonnaise

Toss the ingredients together, add more vegetables if you prefer and then it is done.

Greek salad:

Cos lettuce torn into big chunks
Fetta cheese cubed
Roma tomatoes coarsely diced
Purple Spanish onion sliced
Handful of olives chopped
A cucumber coarsely chopped
Greek salad dressing

Throw it all together with enthusiasm, and enjoy with crusty bread, or serve it on the side.

BRING A PLATE SWEET

5 minutes preparation:

Fruit platter:

Slice up watermelon into small wedges that are easy to hold.

Slice a pineapple longwise into narrow wedges then along the peel, then vertically at 1 cm intervals. Put toothpicks nearby to pull out the individual wedges.

Separate a large bunch of grapes into little bunches of about 4 or 5 grapes.

Make a mixed plate if you prefer cutting apples into wedges without core and wiping with orange wedges to stop browning. Add oranges in wedges with peel on, bananas also need the orange treatment, kiwi fruit are colourful. Strawberries, and cherries, just throw them on.

Fairy bread:

White or wholemeal sandwich bread
Butter or substitute
Nonpareils (hundreds and thousands)

Spread the bread with butter; sprinkle the nonpareils, cut diagonally into triangles. Adults love them as much as children do.

Cheats:

You have had a really busy day, open a pack of good chocolate biscuits onto a plate, slice a bought cake, Madeira or fruit cake are always popular or take a mud cake complete with its container if people know you hate cooking. The pretty plate or glass dish or paper doily will make it look like you put in the effort. All these items disappear really quickly, and are very popular so lose the guilt over not having time to make fairy cakes from scratch.

10-15 minutes preparation:

Caramel tarts see Desserts

Lemon tarts as above.

Marshmallows

1 ½ cups castor sugar
½ cup cold water
4 teaspoons of powdered gelatin
½ cup hot water
1 teaspoon vanilla essence
A few drops food colour if wanted

Coconut or icing sugar to roll in (the marshmallows not you)

Put sugar and cold water in a bowl and use mixer to beat 3 minutes. Sprinkle the gelatin on hot water and stir with fork or whisk until dissolved. Now add gelatin mix while it is still hot to sugar, and beat on high for about 10 minutes until thick and white, add vanilla just before finished. Pour into a chilled tray and refrigerate until set. Cut into cubes with a wet knife and roll marshmallows in icing sugar or coconut.

20-30 minutes preparation:

Little apple turnovers see Spinach and ricotta triangles.

Berry triangles see Spinach and ricotta triangles.

Mini muffins see cakes.

Lemon and poppy seed muffins

BRING A PLATE SAVOURY

5 minutes preparation:

Chips

Get nice crisps put them into a big bowl and watch them disappear. Sorry that only takes 20 seconds if you are slow.

Dip

Buy a good dip put it in the centre of a pretty plate, spread a packet of savoury biscuits in a circle around it and make it tidy. Or you could get Jatz and water crackers and put one type on each side.

Grasshoppers:

Celery
Peanut butter
Spread peanut butter into the hollow of the celery and cut into 10 cm lengths, healthy, yummy and fast.

Asparagus rolls:

Tin of asparagus spears
1 slice of white or wholemeal bread per spear
Butter or substitute

Cut the crusts off the bread, butter each slice then lay one asparagus spear diagonally on each slice of bread. Roll up starting at the empty corner over to the opposite empty corner and pin with a toothpick.

10 minutes preparation:

Sandwiches of your choice cut diagonally into four. Curried egg, ham with whatever, cheese and most things, salmon, salad (not too full or it will fall out).
Go fancy with one white slice and one wholemeal, cut off the crusts and make 3 strips out of the sandwiches. Now to sell it, some shredded lettuce round the edge of your fancy plate, strategically placed mint or parsley. See you put in the effort and cared, you just still hate cooking and/or are time poor!

Dip and crudités

Buy dip put it in the centre of the plate with its lid still on so others can see what flavour it is.

Cut a selection of carrot sticks, celery sticks, capsicum sticks and cucumber if desired. Spread these in groups round the dip. Add water crackers if needed.

15 minutes preparation:

Heat up party pies and sausage rolls and take them hot. Warm up some of your previously frozen savoury triangles.

30 minutes preparation:

Spinach and ricotta triangles

Makes 54 triangles 9cm long, or 24 standard 15 cm long (pictured)
6 sheets frozen shortcrust or puff pastry if you want them flaky

1 bunch silver beet (spinach)
1 large onion
500g ricotta cheese, full cream or low fat.
1 tablespoon butter

Lay pastry plastic side down on the bench, this will thaw in the time it takes to prepare the filling.
Grease oven sheets (flat oven trays).

Preheat oven to 220°C fan forced, higher for standard.

Wash the silver beet leaving wet, chop the stems finely and put in a large boiler put in butter and finely chopped onion, cook on medium until clear, about a minute. Coarsely chop the green leaves without shaking off the water, drop in on top of the onions etc. Put on the cover. In about 5 minutes the silver beet will be cooked and about half the volume. Stir in the ricotta and remove from heat.

For party sized triangles divide each pastry sheet into 3 across the top and down the sides, cut along these lines into 9 squares. For meal sized cut the pastry into two, giving 4 squares.

Brush milk along the outside edges of the squares, put a pile of filling onto one corner and fold the opposite side over. Press along the joins with fingers then press with fork or spoon to make patterns on the join. Put a cut on the top of each to let the air out, and brush with milk.

Put on tray then into the oven. Remove when brown, about 10 to 15 minutes depending on size.

Alternate fillings:

Leftover savoury mince
Whatever you feel like,
Fruit fresh, stewed or tinned apples, apricots, berries.

Sausage rolls

18 long thin sausages
6 sheets frozen puff pastry
Set oven to 220°C.

Lay puff pastry on bench plastic sheet downwards. Slice each of the pastry sheets into three long rectangles. Slice sausages lengthwise just through the skin. Place each sausage onto a strip of pastry, pull the skin away. Now squish the sausages to the full length of the pastry. Brush one long side of the pastry with milk.

Starting away from the brushed side, curl the pastry over the sausage meat. Roll the pastry over to overlap, press down to seal. Brush the top with milk or beaten egg. Beaten egg gives a rich yellow glaze, milk gives a nice brown top, your choice.

For large sausage rolls cut the roll into two, for party rolls, cut into 6. Place on a greased oven tray, leaving room for expansion. As soon as they are brown on top pull them out and start eating.

Alternate fillings:

Sausage mince with grated vegetables and herbs.
Chicken mince with onion and herbs.
Whatever you feel like, provided it is at least the consistency of sausage mince and will cook thoroughly in the 10-15 minutes in the oven.

BREAKFAST

Breakfast is a time when everyone is hungry now, and unless you are retired a very busy time. So very hungry, much to do, time is short, feed everyone a nourishing breakfast to set them up for the day in less time than it takes to get served at a fast food joint. Therefore each of these with practice can be prepared in less than 5 minutes.

Cereal:

Go for something nutritious such as muesli, weetbix, just right, (I am using lower case as the brand matters not, it is the type of cereal that matters). Do not use corn flakes, rice bubbles or sugary cereals include nutrigrain and milo flakes in this group, as they have too much added salt, yes as much as a packet of crisps, and the sugary cereals have heaps of sugar, more than a chocolate bar in some cases and far too much artificial flavours, colours and preservatives. Many have less nutrition than the box, it, at least has fibre. Well worth checking on the nutritional value of the large brand cereals, use web sites that are not owned by the manufacturer.

Pour prepared cereal into a bowl, now slice banana, strawberries or whatever fruit you like, even open a tin of fruit and put it on top, sprinkle with sunflower kernels or crushed nuts of choice (Brazil nuts will save the Amazon and rain forests and reduce cocaine production). Serve with milk or yoghurt, or milk substitute. Add a drink and you are set.

Porridge: oatmeal

Quick cooking oats ¼ cup per person
½ cup boiling water per person
1 tablespoon of skim milk powder, or substitute per person.

Boil jug of water for tea or coffee and add an extra 2-3 cups of water.

In a pot add oats and powdered milk pour over water as measured and stir over medium heat for 1 minute. When bubbling like thermal pools in the geyser regions remove from heat and serve. Best with a sprinkle of raw sugar and cinnamon and a splash of milk round the side. For those with milk intolerance leave out the powdered milk and serve with substitute of choice, or use hot substitute milk instead of milk powder and water.

Very yummy variations:

Add a handful of sultanas with the oats before cooking
Add a handful of dried apricots to the oats before cooking
My favourite add a chopped apple, a tablespoon of sultanas to the oats before cooking, sprinkle with sunflower kernels, raw sugar, and cinnamon before splashing the milk around. You should not be hungry again until lunch.

Eggs:

Egg and soldiers.

Soft boil an egg, (put egg into a pot, cover with water, bring to the boil, then keep boiling for 2 minutes) serve in an egg cup with wholemeal toast cut into fingers to dip.

Scrambled eggs

1-2 eggs per person and same volume of milk
Parsley to serve or include or both
1 teaspoon of butter to grease pot
Break eggs into pot, fill to the same depth with milk. Using a balloon whisk or a fork, whisk vigorously until an even colour. On moderate heat stir slowly until set, about 2-3 minutes. Serve with toast, or on toast, decorate with parsley.

Variations

A little finely chopped onion and tomato
Some grated cheese
Finely chopped chives with or without grated cheese
Left over chopped ham or a little bacon.

Fried eggs

1 or 2 eggs per person, cooking spray/ margarine/ butter
Toast to serve, cook simultaneously.

In a large pan put the required number of egg rings if using, spray egg rings and pan together. When the pan is medium hot, crack the eggs one at a time into the egg rings. For sunny side up cover with a lid to cook both sides at once or turn over as they start to set.

To cheer things up draw a smiley face with sauce on the individual eggs sitting on their individual toast slices.

Wholemeal is best, anything is better than plain white bread.

Toasted eggs

Toasted eggs

Use an egg ring to cut the centre out of a slice of bread, keep the centre. Grease a pan on med-hot. Lay slices of bread, two at a time, on the pan, use an electric frying pan for a family. Break an egg into each hole; place the circles of bread to cook in the pan at the same time. Turn the bread over as it browns, 30 seconds should finish the cooking on the other side. Lay the toast with egg on the plate and rest the cut out on top of the egg.

Egg bread / French toast.

1 egg for every 2 slices of toast
Volume of eggs in milk
Butter for frying or spray oil.

Beat eggs and milk together with fork or whisk until evenly mixed. Using a fork, skewer a slice of bread and coat both sides with the egg mixture. Fry in a thin layer of butter on med-high or spray pan for low fat. Brown then turn over, brown the other side. Breakfast is ready.

Baked beans on toast

1 tin baked beans
Bread
Remove baked beans from tin, heat in a pot on the stove, it is quicker than the microwave for this, serve on toast.

Jaffles

If they are running late and need to take breakfast with them serve on a piece of paper towel, with a popper or juice.

2-4 slices of bread per person
1 slice of cheese for 2 slices of bread
2 slices of tomato per 2 slices of toast

Heat the sandwich press. Butter the bread and put the buttered side out and the filling in the middle. Put in sandwich press until brown.

Alternate fillings

Leftover spaghetti bolognese mince
Leftover stew, any sort, not runny
Sliced cold sausages with chutney
Leftover roast
Plain cheese
Cheese tomato and onion
Asparagus and cheese

Pancakes

One plastic bottle of pancake mix, add water and shake, pour onto a preheated medium pan, that is, well-greased. Pour about ¼ cup each time, as bubbles form and burst turn over, then about 10 seconds later drop pancake onto plate.

Serve with choice of topping; I prefer a squeeze of fresh orange and a teaspoon of raw sugar shaken over.

If you plan ahead and mix this the night before, or have an extra half an hour before to let the mixture rest use this recipe, it tastes lovely and has no artificial flavours colours or preservatives, and you know exactly what is in it!

Pancakes made properly but fast

1 teaspoon of melted butter /or soft margarine
1 big egg
1 ½ cups of milk
1 ½ cups self-raising flour
2 tablespoons of sugar
Splash of vanilla
1 orange cut in half
Sugar to sprinkle

Using a whisk, mix butter, milk and egg with vanilla until an even colour. Throw in the flour and sugar, give it a flick around. It is ready to use now, but if you leave it in the fridge for half an hour, or overnight if morning is too busy, then the pancakes will be fluffier. This should have taken less than 3 minutes. If you want to bump the fibre in meals without it being obvious, add a couple of tablespoons of oat bran. This is supposed to lower cholesterol, it is worth a try, to add extra calcium make the milk with double strength skim milk powder.

Pour about ¼ cup each time. As bubbles form and burst turn over, then about 10 seconds later drop pancake onto plate.

Serve with choice of topping, I prefer a squeeze of fresh orange and a teaspoon of raw sugar shaken over.

Variations

Add a mashed banana or grated apple and cinnamon to the mixture

COOKING FOR FOOD INTOLERANCES

Lactose free:

Any of the previous recipes that do not use any manufactured foods and substitute for the milk, cream or cheese.

Stick to fresh fruit, vegetables and meat and you do not have to substitute anything! It is also better for everyone.

I love this cake recipe, no eggs, no soy, no gluten, no sugar, no lactose, I thought I was doing really well with that until a person with pineapple allergy came for afternoon tea. Always ask about food intolerances, people will not always tell you beforehand if they do not want to make a fuss, but you feel bad if they cannot eat anything. It is worse if they have to bring their own.

Small tin of crushed pineapple in juice
1 cup desiccated coconut
Raw sugar if wanted, probably not, it is great without
One cup of self raising flour or 1 ¼ cup gluten free flour.

Stir until mixed, slop into greased cup cake pans, cook in a moderate oven until brown. They do keep for a few days, but only if no one is at home.

For gluten free do not serve anything that you have thickened, no flour, bread or pre mixed icing, or pastry or pasta. Unless you buy specific gluten free items, but even those have been known to have the allergens in them.

To substitute for eggs:

1. if the eggs are used as binding 1/4 cup of apple puree per egg up to 2 eggs or 1/4 cup mashed banana or similar fruit.
2. if the eggs are to aid in rising 1 1/2 tablespoons vegetable oil, 1 1/2 water, 1 teaspoon baking powder (check for gluten if intolerant) per egg used or 1 teaspoon baking soda (bicarb) , 1 tablespoon white vinegar per egg or if not lactose intolerant 3/4 cup low fat yoghurt for 2 eggs
3. either, 1 tablespoon powdered flax seed mixed with 3 tablespoons warm water, let it stand a minute or two before.

WARNING MANY COMMERCIAL EGG SUBSTITUTES ARE MADE FROM EGGS!!!!!!!!!!!!!!!!!!

Gluten free flour substitutes, rice flour, and tapioca starch or potato starch mixed in roughly 1:1:1 will work but you will need to experiment. Again read the packets carefully if you are allergic and are unsure do not use it!

Nut allergies; be very careful with anything frozen or in a packet. The item may be nut free but made in a factory with nuts and has become contaminated. Stick to fresh fruits, vegetables, meats and cook it yourself.

Converting recipes to low fat/ low sugar.

Lower fat is done simply - substitute skim milk powder made triple strength for cream.

Spray oil on a tray or pan rather than deep or shallow fry.

Do not use pastry.

Steam potatoes, cut into wedges, when tender, spray with oil and oven roast for a few minutes until brown. Taste like roast potatoes and look like roast potatoes.

Cook your own do not buy pre-packaged foods. Many have lots of hidden fat and sugar and salt to make the stuff taste tolerable after too long on the shelves.

Use fresh fruit and vegetables, and grill meats of all sorts.

Use herbs and spices for flavour.

Reduce salt or eliminate it and everyone can choose to add salt at the table or leave it off completely.

Reduce sugar -sweet treats are just that, treats, not part of a well-balanced meal. When cooking fruit (only if you just do not want it raw and tasty) do not add sugar, instead only use ripe fruit in season when it is in its most abundant, cheapest and sweetest. Sugar is necessary as a preservative if bottling fruit but not if you eat it straight away or freeze it. Let's face it if you were going to bottle fruit and spend days in the kitchen would this book appeal to you?

Definitely do not add sugar substitute, research has shown it actually increases sugar cravings and is no more helpful for diabetics than a properly planned diet with balance. Some research has even indicated it is positively dangerous.

Do not have soft drinks (sodas). So easy. Most have even had caffeine added to them to make them addictive and to make you thirstier. They do not quench your thirst but they do make you thirstier, probably best if you avoid them completely, or use just at celebrations interspersed with lots of water.

If you are having chocolate, and I do, regularly, have dark chocolate and no gooey fillings, it just has less sugar. Lots less.

Have fruit as a between meal snack, and have sufficient meat and vegetables at meals so that you are not hungry. If you think you are hungry, have a glass of water, you are more likely thirsty. If you are still hungry 10 minutes later have fruit or carrot sticks.

Faster Still

Whenever you are making something for dinner double or treble the quantities.

A tossed salad will last 2 days in the refrigerator if you leave the dressing off and put in a serving bowl with cling wrap, or a plastic container with lid for a picnic the next day. Add the dressing just before serving.

With a quiche, cook in individual serving dishes if you live alone, or a family sized dish, if not, and freeze the second or third quiche for when you are tired, in a hurry or cannot be bothered. This reduces the power consumption from individually cooking them in the oven.

When making savoury mince for spaghetti bolognese make extra and use it as the base for a shepherd's pie, spice some up for tacos. Little bits left over are lovely in jaffles, in a sandwich press.

Extra cooked vegetables are great in the quiche recipe, or mashed on top of a shepherd's pie, see above.

A quick omelet with tossed salad can be prepared in less than 15 minutes, tastes great and is really healthy, add wholemeal French bread stick that was pre sliced and conveniently in the freezer. The bread will thaw on the bench in the time the salad is prepared.

When cooking cakes and biscuits, always pop a few freezer bags with 6 into the freezer for thawing later in the 10 minutes on the bench whilst you prepare a lovely cup of tea in nice china. Expect compliments because presentation counts, you eat with your eyes as much as with your mouth. Just look at how many people photograph their meal when dining out.

GETTING CHILDREN TO EAT
(without tears – yours or theirs)

Make it pretty!

Dragonfly

Sunflower

For apple and banana pieces, unless it is going to be eaten within five minutes, wipe an orange segment over the cut surfaces to stop it going brown.

This took me 2 minutes to do, time well spent, that included both sunflowers and wiping over with juice. You will notice that all the segments are not perfect, nor precise and no photo stylist was used. This is this far more real than reality food shows. Good is lovely, perfect adds undue stress without improvement of outcomes.

Cut an apple into wedges, remove core
Cut the green off a strawberry (hull)
Cut an orange into wedges or a peeled banana into circles
Snow peas or string beans for stem and leaves
Make your flower on a plastic plate and take it outside for a picnic.
Substitute whatever fruits or vegetables are in season

Egg Boats

1 hard-boiled egg
½ cheese slice cut diagonally into 2 triangles not cheese spread slices unless there is nothing else in the house they tend to be a bit limp. Or better still a slice of block cheese cut diagonally into 2 triangles
1 lettuce leaf
1 piece of dry spaghetti.

Slice egg long wise in two, slice a little of the white in the middle so it has a flat surface to rest on.

Put lettuce on a plate rest two eggs yolk upwards.
Put a piece of the spaghetti as a mast through the cheese to make a sail, triangles are easy but so are rectangles that are slightly bowed, all look fun. Get the children to help. Adults like these too!

You can put fish in the water (lettuce).

If you want to make 2 fish as well:
1 roma tomato
A few thin slices of carrot
Slice roma tomato lengthwise, put cut side down.

Cut fins and tail from thin slices of carrot or cucumber or any other vegetable in the fridge.

Make it quickly; make it fun, if you have fun they will too. It helps if you are snacking on the leftover vegetables, they will want to as well. Get them to help and design their own. Remember the aim is fun not perfection.

Cut wholemeal bread into triangles party style, with a scrape of vegemite, peanut butter, tomato paste with cheese or other healthy spread, leave off the butter they do not need the extra fat. Use the bread to decorate the boats and fish as rocks.

If the darlings do not wish to eat do not give filling things like muesli bars, or biscuits or cakes (high sugar and fat) between meals. If they are hungry they will eat unless you get stressed if they don't. This is something that they can control in their world. Most parents learn that too late to be useful to their own children but early enough for grandchildren.

Make it Fun

Make mini pizzas out of half wholemeal muffins, mini pita bread or standard wholemeal bread slices, cut in circles with an egg ring if they do not want squares. Use tomato paste, basil, oregano, a hint of garlic on the base then as many different vegetables and some meat or fish, cover with grated low fat cheese, oven bake or grill. Obviously you double the quantities so next time they just jump out of the freezer.

Hide the Fruit and Vegetables

Grate carrots, throw in some peas and corn and any leftover vegetables into your spaghetti sauce. Hide vegetables in meatloaf, meatballs, meat pies, sausage rolls, if they like to eat it hide extra vegetables in it! Macaroni cheese should never be all white, layer tomatoes, onions, throw in peas and corn, while you are at it make the cheese sauce with triple strength skim milk powder so it tastes creamy and has all that extra nutrition.

Make mini muffins as snack foods, use peas, corn, grated carrots, onion, capsicum, zucchini, herbs and grated cheese and lose the sugar in a standard muffin recipe. They taste great and look colourful, freeze well, and travel well in the freezer. Did I mention how quick and easy they were to make? See muffin recipe.

Hide fruit in smoothies, pureed in ice block moulds as ice blocks, and make fruit the only snack all chopped up that you take for both of you when you go to the park. Fresh air encourages an appetite.

Sauce Works

Cheese sauce over any vegetable, tomato sauce (watch labels for salt and sugar content) over anything, reduce it as they get a taste for the food underneath. Let them be the ones to add the sauce or not.

Custard made at home with low sugar content and triple strength powdered milk covers any fruit, however some toddlers will eat vegetables with custard, if it works to get them to eat, go for it. They will grow out of it as they see that others do not do it, but in the meantime they eat the vegetables, get extra protein and calcium. Win-win.

Picnics and Parties for Teddy and Dolly

If they do not want lunch at all, agree with them, and have a picnic for teddy and dolly. Invite them, have party food, see make it fun for ideas. The only rule is make everything worth eating for them. No junk food if they do not want to eat, it defeats the purpose and takes away their limited appetite. The back yard works well, so does the fort in the park, on a blanket near the swings, or on the lounge room floor on a blanket if it is raining or too cold to go out.

YOUR OWN RECIPES

www.ingramcontent.com/pod-product-compliance
Lightning Source LLC
Chambersburg PA
CBHW070546300426
44113CB00011B/1807